ANIMAL
SUPERSTARS

WRITTEN BY **JINNY JOHNSON**
ILLUSTRATED BY
MICHAEL WOODS AND **TUDOR HUMPHRIES**

MARSHALL PUBLISHING • LONDON

A Marshall Edition
Conceived, edited and designed by
Marshall Editions
170 Piccadilly, London W1V 9DD

First published in the UK in 1997 by Marshall Publishing Ltd.

Copyright © 1997 Marshall Editions Developments Ltd.

ISBN: 1-84028-048-4

Managing Editor:
Kate Phelps
Designers:
Ian Winton
Ed Simkins
Art Director:
Branka Surla
Editorial Director:
Cynthia O'Brien

Originated by Fotographics
UK/Hong Kong
Printed and bound in Portugal by
Printer Portuguesa

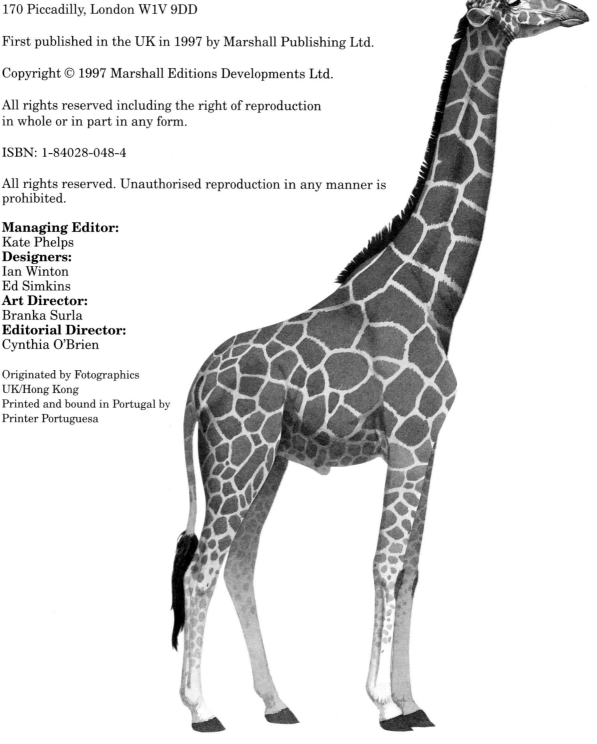

Contents

Which are the biggest insects? 6

How big is the biggest butterfly? 8

Which is the biggest spider? 10

Which is the biggest bird? 12

Which bird has the biggest wings? 14

Which bird has the biggest nest? 16

How big is the biggest fish? 18

Which is the longest snake? 20

How big is the biggest big cat? 22

How tall is a giraffe? 24

How big is an elephant? 26

How big is a whale? 28

How fast can a racehorse run? 30

How fast is a cheetah? 32

How slow is a sloth? 34

How far can a kangaroo jump? 36

How fast can insects and
   spiders move? 38

How far can insects jump? 40

How fast can a snake wriggle? 42

Which is the fastest sea creature? 44

Which is the fastest whale? 46

How fast can birds fly? 48

How fast can a bird run? 50

Which animal wins the race? 52

Questions and answers on:

Animal senses 54

How animals look 56

Animal homes and nests 58

Animal parents 60

Dangerous animals 62

Nature's giants 64

Animal eating habits 66

Animal behaviour 68

Index 70

Which are the biggest insects?

The longest of all insects is a type of stick insect that lives in the hot jungles of Southeast Asia. Other big insects are the giant beetles that live in South American jungles. These include the hercules beetle, which is up to 19 centimetres long – about the same length as a banana.

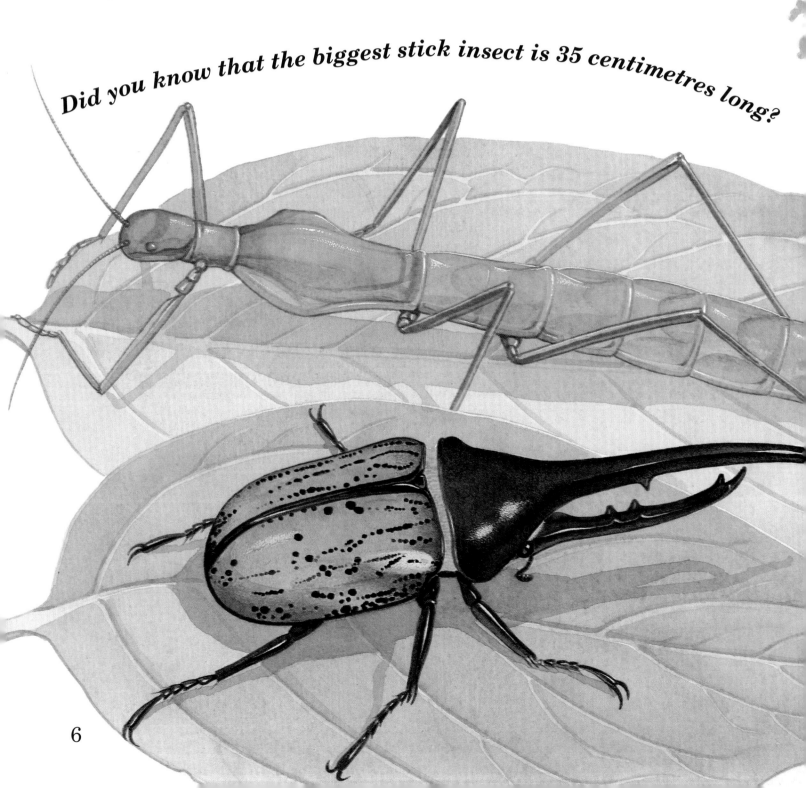

Did you know that the biggest stick insect is 35 centimetres long?

With its long slender body, the stick insect looks just like another twig as it sits in a tree. This helps keep it hidden from hunters such as birds.

The longest stick insect is nearly as long as a child's arm. Can you find the stick insect and child hidden here?

Male hercules beetles have long horns that are the same length as their bodies. They use these horns in battles with other males.

How big is the biggest butterfly?

Some of the largest of all butterflies are the birdwings which live in jungles. Biggest of all is the female Queen Alexandra's birdwing, which measures up to 28 centimetres across with its wings fully spread. The male is smaller than the female and more brightly coloured.

Tiny butterflies such as the Sonoran blue (above) and the Cassius blue (below) measure less than two centimetres across. But some moths are so small that several could fit on your fingernail.

The Queen Alexandra's birdwing is much bigger than an average-sized butterfly such as a red admiral. Can you find the eight red admirals hidden in the birdwing?

Birdwing butterflies live high in jungle trees where they eat nectar – a sugary liquid made by flowers. These beautiful butterflies are now very rare and it is against the law to take them from the wild.

Did you know that a Queen Alexandra's birdwing butterfly is this big?

A red admiral butterfly measures about five centimetres across.

9

Which is the biggest spider?

The giant of the spider world is the female goliath bird-eating spider. Her hairy body measures more than 10 centimetres and her legs spread across 26 centimetres. The male is a little smaller. These spiders live in the jungles of South America. They stay hidden under leaves and stones during the day and come out at night to hunt.

A bird-eating spider is bigger than a bird such as a wren. A wren is about 10 centimetres long.

Although this spider is called a bird-eating spider, it probably catches more snakes, lizards and frogs than birds.

The goliath bird-eating spider weighs about 100 grams. It is almost as heavy as an apple.

Did you know that a goliath bird-eating spider is this big?

A common house spider in Europe and North America is usually about two centimetres long. It is tiny compared to the bird-eating spider.

11

Which is the biggest bird?

The ostrich is the biggest of all birds. It stands more than two and a half metres high, much taller than an adult human, and weighs more than 150 kilograms. Even its eye is bigger than the world's smallest bird – the bee hummingbird.

A male bee hummingbird is only a little more than five centimetres long. Can you see one hidden in the eye of the ostrich?

Although the ostrich has wings it cannot fly. Its body is too big and heavy to lift into the air. But it is a fast runner. It can race along at more than 70 kilometres an hour – faster than any other bird can run.

A female ostrich lays the biggest eggs of any living creature. An ostrich egg can weigh more than one and a half kilograms.

An ostrich egg is up to 16 centimetres long. A hen's egg is much smaller – it is only about six centimetres long.

Did you know that an ostrich's egg is this big?

The egg of the bee hummingbird is the smallest laid by any bird. This tiny egg is less than one centimetre long.

Which bird has the biggest wings?

The wandering albatross has longer wings than any other bird. When fully spread, its wings measure about three and a half metres from tip to tip. Its long wings help the albatross soar for miles over the southern oceans as it searches for food.

Can you find the three five-year-olds hidden on the wings of the albatross? They show just how huge this bird is.

Did you know that the wandering albatross can fly nearly 500 kilometres a day on its huge wings?

Fish and squid are the main foods of the wandering albatross. The bird swoops down to the sea to seize its prey. It also follows ships and picks up food that is thrown overboard as rubbish.

The wandering albatross spends most of its life in the air. It comes to land only to lay its eggs and care for its young.

A common pigeon, or rock dove, looks small next to the huge albatross. Its wings measure about 60 centimetres from tip to tip.

15

Which bird has the biggest nest?

The largest tree nests are made by bald eagles. The biggest ever seen was over two and a half metres wide and six metres deep. The bald eagle builds its nest with sticks and branches and lines it with grass.

Bald eagles catch fish to eat as well as birds and small animals. First the eagle watches until it spots a fish in the water. Then it swoops low and seizes the fish in its strong claws.

Both the male and female bald eagles are kept busy bringing food to their hungry young in the nest.

Did you know that a giraffe could fit into the biggest bald eagle's nest?

Bald eagles do not live in their nest all year round. They use it as a safe place in which to lay their eggs and keep their young. Nests are often used year after year. Each time more twigs and sticks are added.

The tiniest nest of all is made by the bee hummingbird. Its nest is only two and a half centimetres wide – about the size it is shown here.

17

How big is the biggest fish?

The largest fish in the world is the whale shark. The biggest one ever measured was more than 12 metres long and probably weighed as much as 15 tonnes – more than three elephants.

Great white sharks are much smaller than whale sharks, but they are the largest of the fierce, hunting sharks.

Did you know that the biggest whale shark i

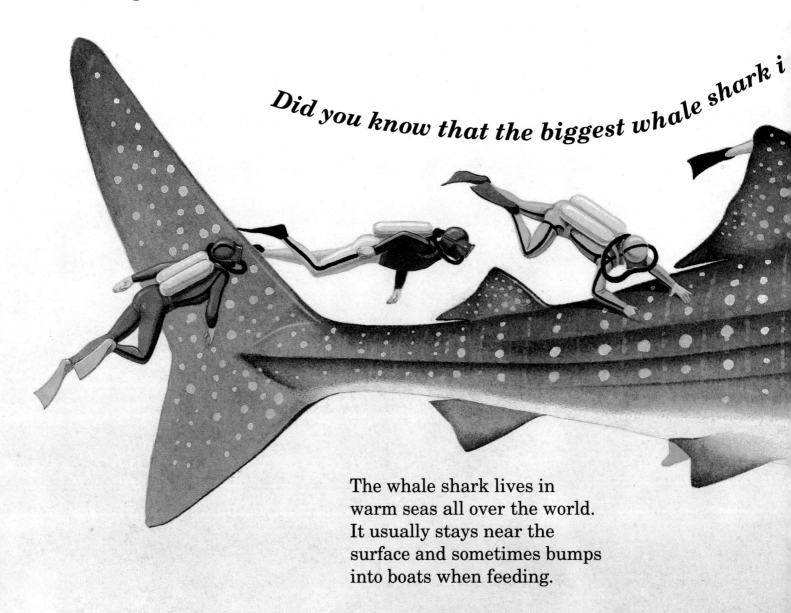

The whale shark lives in warm seas all over the world. It usually stays near the surface and sometimes bumps into boats when feeding.

The whale shark is not a dangerous hunter like most other sharks. When feeding, the whale shark opens its mouth wide to take in lots of tiny fish and shrimps as well as sea water. When the shark closes its mouth again, the water drains out through the slits at the sides of its head, leaving the food behind.

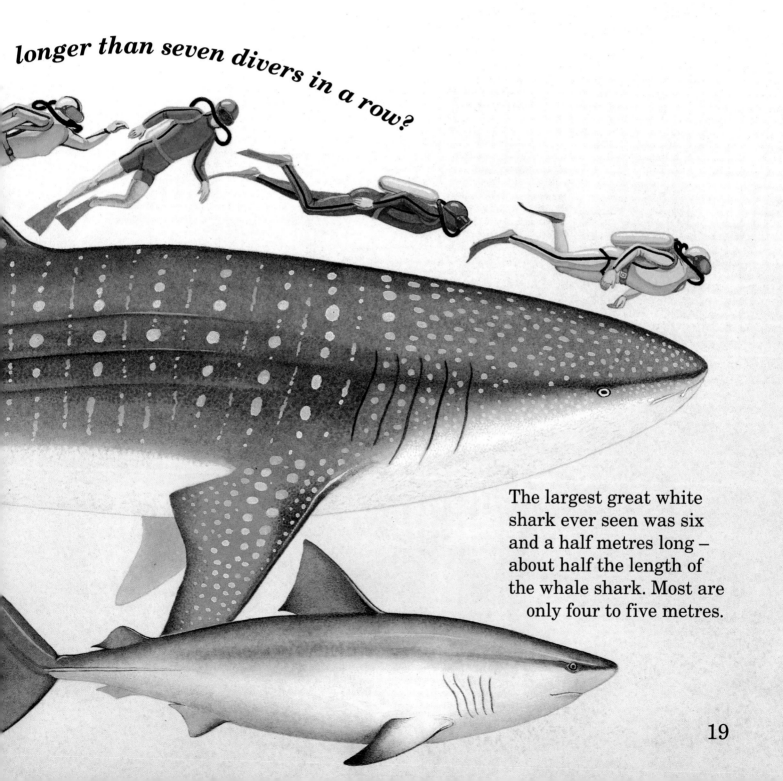

longer than seven divers in a row?

The largest great white shark ever seen was six and a half metres long – about half the length of the whale shark. Most are only four to five metres.

Which is the longest snake?

The longest of all snakes is the reticulated python. Most are more than six metres long, but the biggest python ever seen measured nearly ten metres – nearly as long as three cars. The python is not a poisonous snake. It kills the animals it catches by wrapping them in its strong body until they are crushed to death.

The reticulated python spends the day resting and hunts for food after dark.

Pythons swallow their food whole. After eating a really big meal, such as an antelope, a python may not need to hunt again for several weeks.

Can you find the car hidden in the picture? It shows just how big this snake can be.

Did you know that the reticulated python's body is more than 75 centimetres thick?

How big is the biggest big cat?

The tiger is the biggest of all cats. It measures more than three metres from its nose to the tip of its tail. Not all tigers live in hot jungles. The biggest live in snowy Siberia, which is part of Russia.

Tiger cubs usually stay with their mother for several years. During this time, the cubs learn how to hunt and take care of themselves.

Just like a pet cat stalking a bird, a hunting tiger creeps up on animals such as deer and wild pigs. When the tiger has got as close as possible, it pounces on its prey.

Did you know that a Siberian tiger weighs more than 250 kilograms – as much as 65 pet cats?

A tiger's stripes help keep it hidden in grass and leaves when it is hunting.

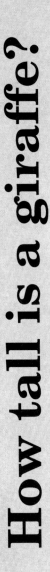

How tall is a giraffe?

The giraffe is the tallest of all land animals. A male giraffe can measure up to six metres from its feet to the horns on the top of its head.

Because giraffes are so tall, they can eat leaves at the tops of trees that other animals cannot reach. The giraffe strips leaves, buds and fruit off trees with its lips and long tongue. A giraffe's tongue measures more than 40 centimetres – it is almost as long as the arm of an adult person.

Giraffes have good eyesight. This helps them watch out for enemies such as lions. They defend themselves by kicking out with their big hooves.

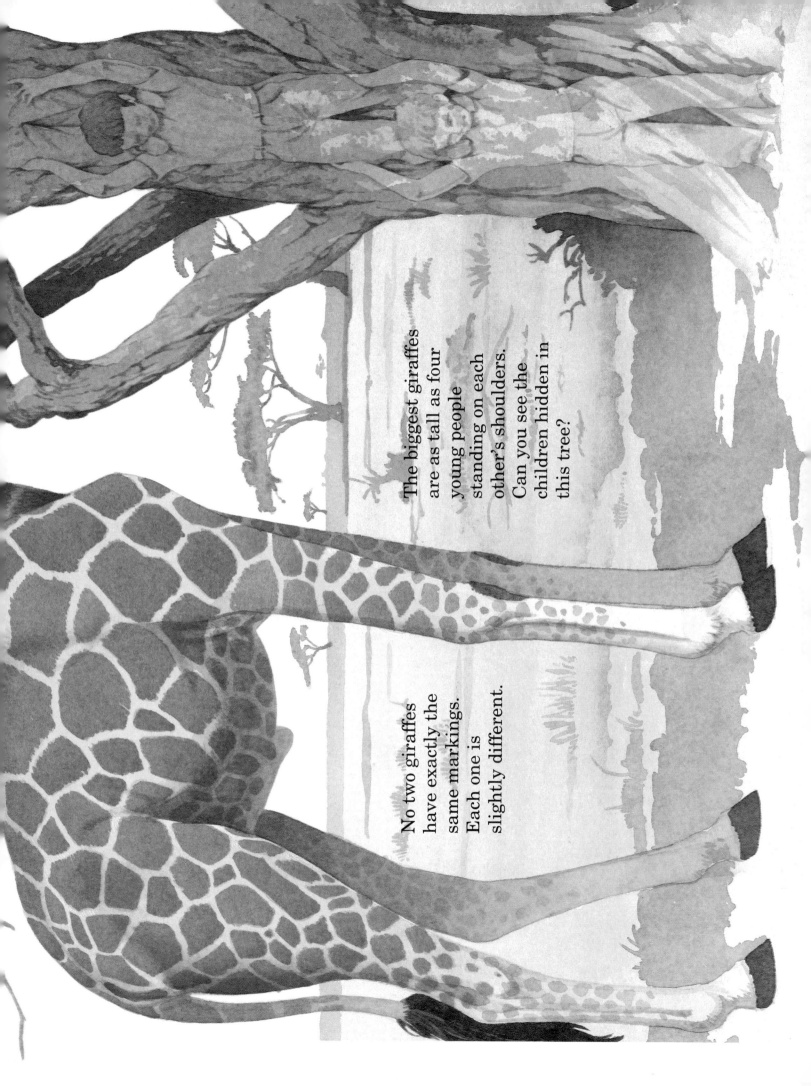

The biggest giraffes are as tall as four young people standing on each other's shoulders. Can you see the children hidden in this tree?

No two giraffes have exactly the same markings. Each one is slightly different.

How big is an elephant?

The African elephant is the biggest land animal alive today. An elephant's tusk alone is as heavy as an adult person. A male elephant weighs about five tonnes. Females are smaller – about half the weight of males.

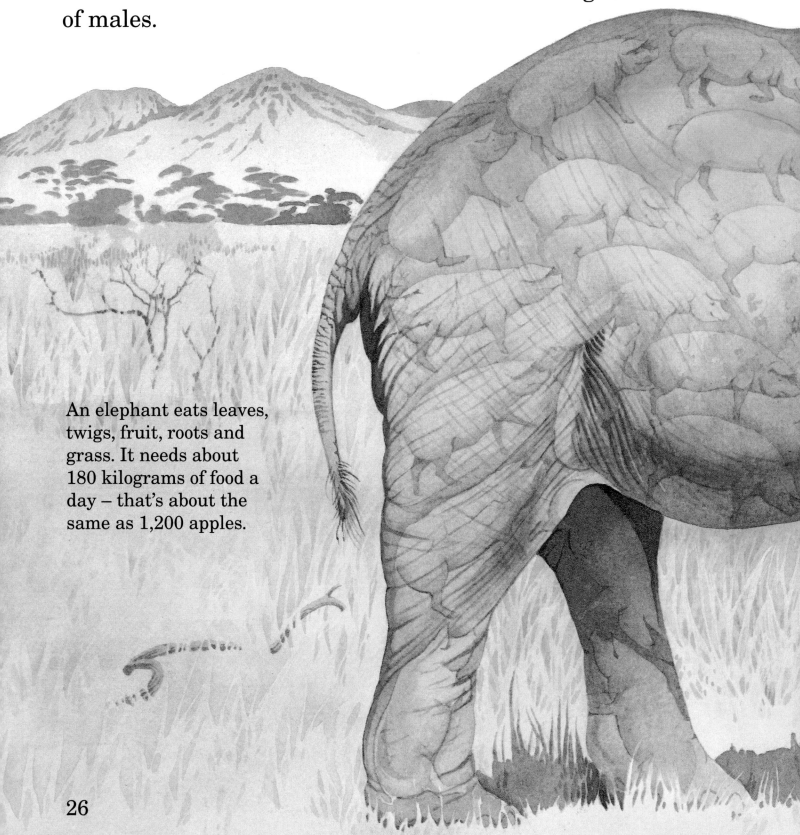

An elephant eats leaves, twigs, fruit, roots and grass. It needs about 180 kilograms of food a day – that's about the same as 1,200 apples.

Even though they are very big, elephants are gentle animals. Mothers and young stay together in herds.

Did you know that an elephant weighs as much as 35 pigs?

An elephant has a trunk instead of a nose. The trunk is used for many things, including smelling, drinking, gathering food and stroking young.

How big is a whale?

The blue whale is the biggest animal that has ever lived. A full-grown blue whale is about 30 metres long, and its tongue alone is heavier than an elephant. Although blue whales are so huge, they eat only tiny shrimps called krill. One blue whale eats about four million of these shrimps every day.

A baby blue whale is bigger than any other baby animal. A newborn blue whale is seven or eight metres long – about the length of two cars. It drinks more than 500 litres of milk a day.

A blue whale can make a louder sound than any other creature. Its whistle is louder than a jet plane.

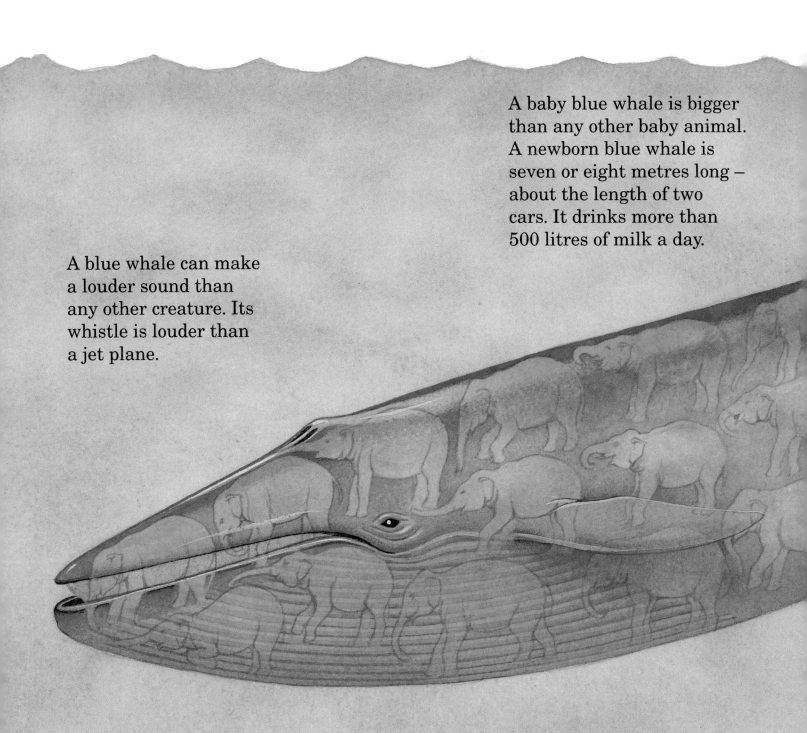

28

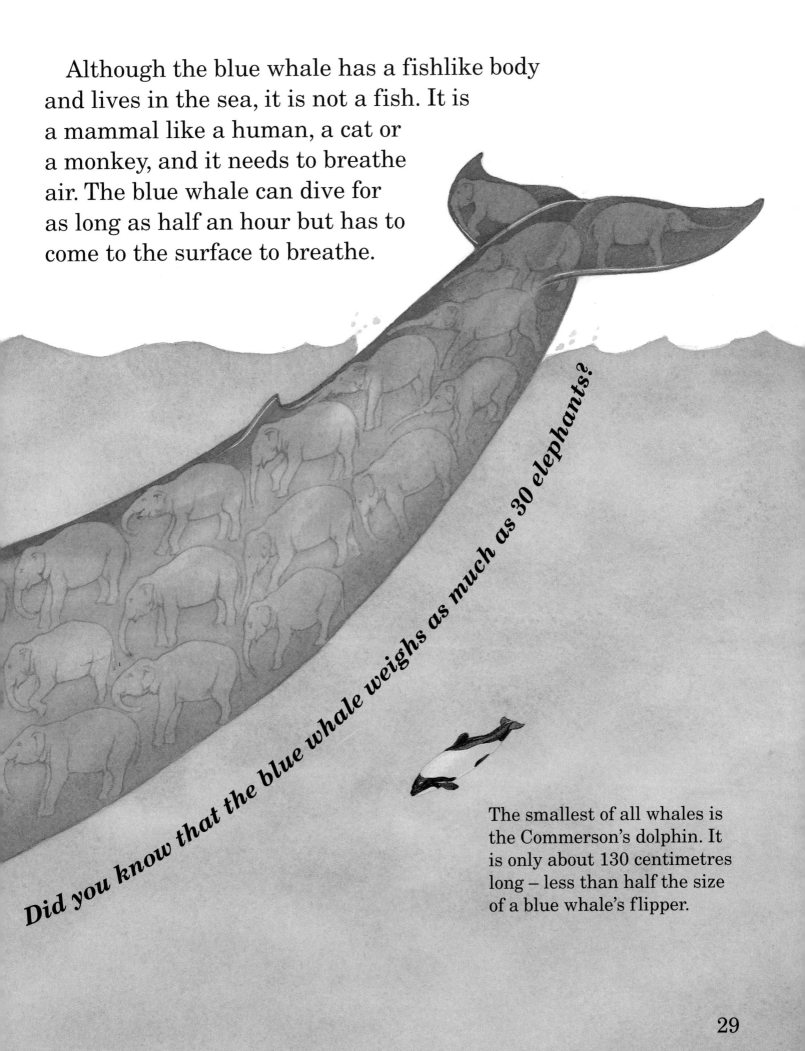

Although the blue whale has a fishlike body and lives in the sea, it is not a fish. It is a mammal like a human, a cat or a monkey, and it needs to breathe air. The blue whale can dive for as long as half an hour but has to come to the surface to breathe.

Did you know that the blue whale weighs as much as 30 elephants?

The smallest of all whales is the Commerson's dolphin. It is only about 130 centimetres long – less than half the size of a blue whale's flipper.

29

How fast can a racehorse run?

The best racehorses can run at more than 60 kilometres an hour – faster than most cars go in a city. The fastest a racehorse has ever run is just over 69 kilometres an hour. This was in a short race of 400 metres. Most racehorses belong to a breed of horses called thoroughbreds. They are slender but strong, with long, slim legs.

Olympic athletes run at speeds of 35 kilometres an hour for short distances. They cover a distance of 100 metres – about the length of a football field – in under 10 seconds.

Greyhounds are much faster than human sprinters. The quickest speed for racing greyhounds is more than 60 kilometres an hour.

All of these runners are sprinters. This means they can only keep up these speeds over short distances.

Did you know that a hare can run faster than a racehorse?

A hare can run at up to 72 kilometres an hour. Speed helps it to escape from enemies such as foxes.

31

How fast is a cheetah?

Cheetahs run faster than any other animal. They can race along at up to about 100 kilometres an hour – a good speed for a car. Can you see the car hidden in the sand?

The cheetah is a sprinter. It cannot keep running at this pace for more than a minute or so.

Did you know that a cheetah can go as fast as a car?

The cheetah runs fast to catch animals to eat, such as gazelles, rabbits and even young ostriches. It gets as near to the prey as possible, then chases after it as fast as it can go.

The pronghorn antelope is not quite as fast as the cheetah – but it keeps going for longer. A pronghorn can run at about 60 kilometres an hour for 10 minutes. Even a young pronghorn can outrun a horse.

Pronghorns live in North America and cheetahs live in Africa, so the two would never meet in the wild.

A pronghorn runs to escape from enemies such as mountain lions and wolves.

How slow is a sloth?

The sloth is one of the slowest of all land animals. It lives in the South American jungle where it hangs upside down from a branch of a tree. From time to time, it pulls itself along the branch to look for leaves to eat.

The giant tortoise takes about a minute to move only six metres. A child could walk that distance in a few seconds. Can you see the children hidden here?

Once a week the sloth climbs down to the ground where it travels even more slowly than it does in the trees. It drags itself along at about two metres a minute.

Did you know that a sloth moves along branches at less than five metres a minute?

The garden snail is even slower than the sloth and the giant tortoise. It takes about an hour to travel 15 metres. That is about twice the width of a tennis court.

35

How far can a kangaroo jump?

Kangaroos are champion jumpers. They travel at up to 40 kilometres an hour by leaping along on their strong back legs. Kangaroos live in Australia, and many of them spend most of their time in the desert. They may need to travel 30 kilometres for a drink of water so moving quickly is important.

The springbok is a kind of gazelle and it is a good jumper, too. If frightened by a lion or other enemy, it leaps high into the air.

The longest a red kangaroo has jumped is more than 12 metres in one bound. This is as long as nine children lying down. Can you find the children hidden in the sand?

Did you know that a kangaroo can jump more than 12 metres?

A grey kangaroo has leapt two and a half metres – as high as two seven-year-old children standing on each other's shoulders. Can you see the children hidden in the bush?

A springbok can leap more than two metres into the air. This leaping is known as pronking or stotting and warns other members of the herd that danger is near.

How fast can insects and spiders move?

Although insects are small they can travel at surprisingly fast speeds. Cockroaches are among the quickest. They have wings but do not use them often. Instead, they scurry along on their long legs.

Some kinds of cockroaches can move at about four kilometres an hour.

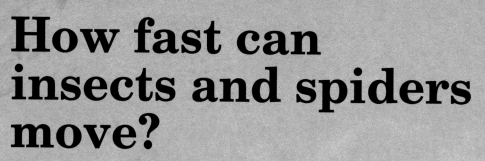

Fast-moving sunspiders are related to spiders and scorpions. They are sometimes called windscorpions because they run like the wind. Sunspiders live in hot, dry places. They catch insects and other small creatures to eat.

Cockroaches stay hidden during the day. At night, they come out to look for food. They eat almost anything – even paper.

Speedy sunspiders run at more than 16 kilometres an hour – probably faster than you can rollerskate.

Did you know that a sunspider can run faster than you?

How far can insects jump?

One champion jumper in the insect world is the click beetle. It can jump as high as 30 centimetres – more than 25 times its own length. The click beetle jumps to escape from its enemies.

The click beetle is only about a centimetre long, but it springs into the air with greater force for its size than a space rocket taking off from earth.

The clicking sound it makes as it leaps into the air gives the click beetle its name.

The tiny flea is another record breaker. It can leap more than 150 times its own length. If a human being could do this, he or she would be able to jump from the ground to the top of a skyscraper.

A flea lives in the fur of an animal such as a cat. Fleas are only a couple of millimetres long. Here a flea is seen through a magnifying glass.

Did you know that a flea can leap up to 20 centimetres?

How fast can a snake wriggle?

Even though snakes don't have legs, they move surprisingly quickly. The black mamba, which lives in Africa, travels along the ground or a tree branch at about 10 kilometres an hour. But it can move at nearly 20 kilometres an hour for short bursts.

Did you know that the black mamba is the fastest of all snakes?

The sidewinder snake moves more slowly than the mamba at about six kilometres an hour. It travels along with a strange sideways motion, leaving a row of marks in the sand.

42

The fastest-moving lizard is the six-lined racerunner. This long, slim lizard can run at up to 28 kilometres an hour – much quicker than the fastest snake. It runs to catch prey such as insects, spiders and scorpions.

The racerunner lizard and the black mamba can move nearly as fast as a pet cat. Can you find a cat hidden in the sand?

A black mamba measures nearly four metres – more than twice as long as an adult human. It eats birds, lizards, mice and other small creatures which it kills with its poisonous fangs.

The racerunner lizard's speed is useful when it is in danger. It makes a swift dash to the safety of a rock or burrow.

Which is the fastest sea creature?

Water is many times thicker than air, so sea creatures have to work much harder than land animals to move fast. They have to push themselves through the water with flippers and fins. It is difficult to measure how quickly sea creatures move, but people think the sailfish is the fastest swimmer.

The gentoo penguin is the fastest-swimming bird. It can move at up to 27 kilometres an hour for short distances.

The leatherback is the biggest and the fastest moving of all sea turtles. Its top speed is about 35 kilometres an hour.

The sailfish can probably swim at about 100 kilometres an hour. Most submarines travel at about 65 kilometres an hour. Can you find the submarine hidden in this picture?

Californian sea lions swim faster than any other type of seal. They speed through the water at up to 40 kilometres an hour for short distances.

Did you know that a sailfish can move faster than a submarine?

Which is the fastest whale?

All whales and dolphins have streamlined, torpedo-shaped bodies – an ideal shape for moving quickly in water. The fastest is probably the killer whale, which can swim at a speed of 55 kilometres an hour for a short time. When not hunting, the whale cruises along at about 16 kilometres an hour.

A whale is not a fish but a mammal like a dog or human. A fish swims by moving its tail from side to side. A whale swims by moving its tail up and down.

The squid swims in a different way from most other sea creatures. It shoots jets of water out of its body to propel itself along at up to 32 kilometres an hour.

Killer whales are among the fiercest hunters in the sea. They eat fish, squid, seals and penguins and need to be able to move fast to catch them. Killer whales live and hunt in family groups called pods. A full-grown killer whale measures up to 10 metres – longer than two cars.

Did you know that a whale can move as fast as a windsurfer?

In this picture you are looking up at the whale from underneath. Can you see the windsurfer riding on top of the water?

How fast can birds fly?

Some of the fastest-flying birds are ducks and geese such as the common eider, the spur-winged goose and the red-breasted merganser. All these birds fly at more than 65 kilometres an hour and may even reach speeds of up to 100 kilometres an hour.

Racing pigeons are speedy birds, too. They can fly at 70 to 80 kilometres an hour.

Common eider

Spur-winged goose

The swiftest bird of all is the peregrine falcon. It catches other birds to eat and makes astonishingly fast dives through the air to seize its prey with its hooked claws. Some dives have been timed at more than 180 kilometres an hour. When flying normally, the falcon travels at up to 95 kilometres an hour.

Did you know that a peregrine falcon can dive through the air at more than 180 kilometres an hour?

Red-breasted merganser

Many geese and ducks are strong, fast fliers. They make regular journeys over hundreds of kilometres between winter and summer homes.

At top speed, a peregrine falcon can fly as fast as a small airplane. Can you find the airplane hidden here?

49

How fast can a bird run?

The ostrich is too big to fly but it is a high-speed runner. It travels at speeds of at least 70 kilometres an hour and perhaps as much as 95 kilometres an hour. Its long legs and large strong feet help the ostrich to run fast.

Chickens rarely fly, nor are they very fast runners. They scuttle around at speeds of only a few kilometres an hour.

The greater roadrunner can fly but generally runs instead. It moves at nearly 20 kilometres an hour – faster than most people can run.

It is important for the ostrich to be able to move quickly because it often has to run to escape from enemies such as lions. Also, it lives in dry lands in southern Africa and needs to travel long distances to find plants to eat.

Running at top speed, an ostrich could keep ahead of a racing cyclist.

Did you know that an ostrich can run faster than any other bird?

51

Which animal wins the race?

In a race of all the record breakers in this book, the cheetah would win on land, the sailfish in the sea and the peregrine falcon in the air. Humans would be left behind!

Who would have thought that an ostrich could run as fast as a racehorse? Look at the animals running on land and see what other surprises you can find.

Birds have no rivals in the air. And the swiftest birds can fly as fast as a small airplane.

A human swimmer would be far behind most of these sea creatures. Even a champion can only manage about eight or nine kilometres an hour for short distances.

Questions and answers on animal senses

WHICH BIRD HAS THE BEST EYESIGHT?

Most birds see well, but hunting birds, such as eagles, have excellent sight. They depend on being able to spot prey animals far below on the ground as they soar in the air. An eagle's eyes are bigger than those of an adult human and its eyesight is probably at least twice as sharp as ours. Some scientists think that the eagle may be able to see details in a landscape eight times smaller than humans can manage.

Golden eagle

Red piranha

CAN FISH SMELL?

Yes, they can. Many fish, including sharks, find their food by smell. And fish such as salmon, which travel back to the stream of their birth to lay their eggs, may find their way by smell. Piranha fish hunt in groups and often kill creatures much larger than themselves. Their sense of smell helps them find prey – they can scent even a tiny drop of blood from a wounded animal in the water and go and attack.

IS AN ELECTRIC EEL REALLY ELECTRIC?

This eel is electric – it kills its prey with electric shocks. Much of the eel's body is made up of special muscles which produce these electric shocks. The electric charge is sent into the water where it can stun and kill other fish and frogs. The electric eel lives in rivers in South America.

Electric eel

CAN MOLES SEE?

Moles do have tiny eyes, but they cannot see very well. They can probably only tell whether it is light or dark. Moles spend most of their lives under the ground so they do not need to see well. Instead they get around by their sense of touch. They have lots of tiny hairy bristles on the nose that are sensitive to the slightest movement.

DO DOGS HAVE THE BEST SENSE OF SMELL?

Most mammals have a much better sense of smell than humans. They rely on smell to help them find food and to warn them of danger. They can tell from another animal's smell whether it is a friend or stranger. Dogs have particularly keen noses. Their sense of smell is at least 40 times better than ours.

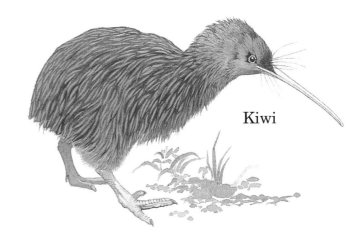

Kiwi

CAN BIRDS SMELL?

Some kinds of vultures, as well as shearwaters and petrels, do have a good sense of smell, but most birds do not. The kiwi is another bird that has a good nose. The nostrils at the tip of its long beak help it to find food such as beetles and worms under several centimetres of earth. The kiwi lives in New Zealand and it cannot fly.

Long-eared bat

DO BATS HAVE SHARP EARS?

Bats can fly and catch insect prey in the air in complete darkness. Their good hearing helps them do this. As it flies, the bat sends out special sound waves that bounce off any object in its way – such as a flying moth. Echoes sent back from the object are picked up by the bat's large ears. The echoes tell the bat about the size and position of the object and so help it find and catch its prey.

CAN OWLS REALLY SEE AT NIGHT?

The owl has large eyes that can see well, even in very dim night light. This helps to make it a good night-time hunter. The owl can also turn its head right round so it can look behind itself. But in complete darkness the owl relies on hearing. Its ears can pick up the slightest sound and tell which direction it is coming from.

Questions and answers on how animals look

WHICH BIRD HAS THE MOST FEATHERS?

The whistling swan has about 25,000 feathers, more than any other bird. The bald eagle, which is well over half its size, has only about 7,000 feathers. Generally, birds which live in cold areas have more feathers than those which live in warm or tropical areas. The bird with the smallest number of feathers counted is the ruby-throated hummingbird, which has only about 1,000.

WHICH ANIMAL HAS THE LONGEST HORNS?

The water buffalo has longer horns than any other animal. Most water buffalo have horns which are each about one metre long, but they can grow to two metres. The water buffalo is used as a farm animal in many parts of the world.

WHICH BIRD HAS THE LONGEST TAIL?

The male crested argus pheasant, which lives in Southeast Asia, has a longer tail than any other bird. It is one and a half metres long and 13 centimetres wide. The male displays his tail to attract females at breeding time.

WHICH ANIMAL HAS THE BIGGEST CLAWS?

The giant armadillo has the longest claws of any animal. Its middle claw is nearly 20 centimetres long. The giant armadillo uses its huge claws to dig into, or smash down, termite mounds. It eats termites, as well as ants and other small creatures.

WHICH MAMMAL HAS THE LONGEST FUR?

The musk ox has an extremely thick coat which keeps it warm in its Arctic home. The outer hairs of its coat grow nearly one metre long and hang down to the ground.

WHICH MAMMAL HAS THE MOST TEETH?

The giant armadillo has about 100 teeth – more than any other land mammal. Many of these drop out before the armadillo is full grown. Of the sea-living mammals, some dolphins have more than 120 teeth.

WHAT ARE A BAT'S WINGS MADE OF?

A bat's wings are very different from the wings of birds. They are made of tiny strips of muscle covered on both sides with skin. The wings are supported on the extra long fingers of the bat's 'hands'.

WHICH BIRD HAS THE LONGEST BEAK?

The beak of the Australian pelican is the longest of any bird. It can be up to 45 centimetres long. The pelican has a large pouch hanging from the lower half of its beak. It uses this pouch to scoop up fish from the water.

Giant armadillo

WHICH SNAKE HAS THE LONGEST FANGS?

The gaboon viper has fangs that are up to five centimetres long, longer than those of any other snake. The fangs are linked to a gland containing strong poison. The viper lives in African rain forests and uses its poisonous fangs to kill prey, such as frogs and ground-living birds.

HOW BIG ARE A SHARK'S TEETH?

The jagged teeth of the great white shark are up to eight centimetres long. A shark may have 3,000 teeth arranged in rows in its mouth. The first row are used for killing prey and eating. The rest are replacements, ready to move into place when front teeth wear out.

WHICH ANIMAL HAS THE LARGEST SHELL?

The giant clam has the biggest shell of any animal. It measures as much as 107 centimetres long. This huge clam lives in the Indian and Pacific oceans. It feeds on plankton – microscopic plants and animals that live in seawater.

Questions and answers on animal homes and nests

DO ANY FISH MAKE NESTS?

Most fish just lay their eggs and leave them to float in the water until they hatch. A few, such as the ballan wrasse, do take more trouble. The male and female wrasse make a nest of weeds, wedged into rocks under the sea. The female lays her eggs in the nest and the male watches over them.

The labyrinth fish lives in rivers. The male blows a nest of bubbles on the surface of the water. The bubbles are made stronger than normal by a special sticky mucus produced by the fish. When the female lays her eggs they float up to the surface of the water into the bubble nest.

Termites

WHICH ANIMAL DIGS THE BIGGEST BURROWS?

Prairie dogs are a kind of rodent. They live in huge groups called colonies and dig lots of connecting burrows, called 'towns'. These prairie dog towns may cover an area as big as more than 80 football fields.

Prairie dog

WHICH INSECT MAKES THE BIGGEST NEST?

Termites are tiny insects that live together in groups called colonies. There may be a million termites in one colony. Termites make nests to live in. Some are round and built on the branches of trees. Others are made on the ground and look like huge towers. These towers can be seven metres tall – higher than four adult people standing on top of one another.

Part of the nest is under the ground. The termites live here and look after their young. The tower on top contains chimneys, which keep air circulating through the nest.

HOW DOES A HARVEST MOUSE MAKE ITS NEST?

The tiny harvest mouse makes a beautiful nest on stems of corn or other tall grasses. She winds one stem around another to make a little platform above the ground. She then takes lengths of grass and carefully weaves the ball-shaped nest. She lines the inside with shredded grass leaves. Her young live in the nest for about three weeks.

DO ALL BIRDS MAKE NESTS IN TREES?

No, many seabirds lay their eggs on a rocky ledge on cliffs or in a dip scraped in the ground. The burrowing owl digs a hole in the ground and the manx shearwater often uses an old rabbit burrow. Most unusual of all is an Australian bird called the mallee fowl. Instead of sitting on its eggs, it makes a mound of rotting plants and covers it with sandy soil. The eggs are laid in a hole in the mound and then covered over. The eggs are kept warm inside the mound until they hatch.

Mallee fowl

WHY DO BEAVERS BUILD DAMS?

Beavers build a dam across a flowing stream to make a wide pond of still water. They live and keep a food store in this pond. Once the stream is dammed with branches and mud, the beavers start to build a lodge to shelter in. The lodge is made from branches and twigs and the outside is plastered with mud. An air hole is left in the top

Beaver

of the lodge. In autumn, the beavers collect lots of branches. They keep these in their food store under the water so that they have plenty of bark to feed on through the cold winter months.

DO ANY REPTILES MAKE NESTS?

Sea-living turtles, such as the green turtle, dig pits in which to keep their eggs safe. When ready to lay her eggs, the female turtle drags herself out of the water and up the beach. She digs a hole with her back flippers and lays about 100 eggs. She covers them over with sand and returns to the sea. When the baby turtles hatch they must make their own way out of the nest and down to the sea.

Questions and answers on animal parents

DO ALL BIRDS FEED THEIR YOUNG?

No – some birds, such as baby ducks and hens, are able to move around and peck for food almost as soon as they hatch. They learn how to find food by following their mothers. But many other birds are born helpless and must be fed by their parents. Eagles and hawks kill prey and bring it to their babies. Small, insect-eating birds such as robins may make up to 60 feeding trips an hour to satisfy hungry mouths.

Indian python

WHICH MAMMAL HAS THE SMALLEST BABIES?

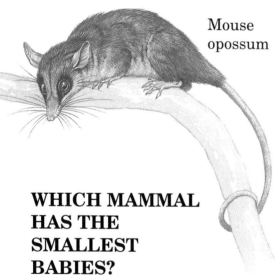

Mouse opossum

The mouse opossum gives birth to some of the smallest babies of any mammal. It lives in the forests of Central and South America and measures 7.5 to 17.5 centimetres long. The babies are only about six millimetres long – not much bigger than a grain of rice. The tiny babies cling to their mother's teats as she moves around the forest.

DO SNAKES LOOK AFTER THEIR YOUNG?

Most snakes do not look after their eggs or young at all. But the python winds her body around her eggs to guard them. She can even shuffle along like this to move the eggs into the early morning sun or into the shade at midday. Once the eggs have hatched she looks after the babies in the same way.

WHICH SPIDER IS THE BEST MOTHER?

The female wolf spider is certainly one of the best. She guards her eggs, and when they hatch, she carries the baby spiders on her back. She may have as many as 40 babies clinging to her body as she moves around looking for food. The spiders stay with her until they are big enough to survive by themselves.

WHICH ANIMAL IS PREGNANT FOR LONGEST?

The female elephant carries her baby for about 22 months. She usually has only one baby at a time – twins are very rare. The baby elephant weighs about 110 kilograms when it is born, almost as much as two adult people. It lives in a family group called a herd with its mother, any older brothers and sisters, and other female elephants. It feeds on its mother's milk for at least two years.

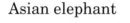

Aphid

Asian elephant

WHICH CREATURE HAS THE MOST BABIES?

Insects can produce large numbers of offspring in a very short time. One aphid on a plant can become a thousand in an afternoon. A queen honeybee or termite produces all of the thousands of insects in her colony. Among mammals, small rodents, such as mice and voles, have the most babies. Voles can produce five or six litters of six or more babies in a year. Of the birds, the grey partridge may have the biggest clutch. It lays as many as 19 eggs at one time.

HOW BIG IS A BABY PANDA?

A full grown panda weighs more than 112 kilograms – twice as much as an adult person. But she gives birth to a baby so tiny that it weighs little more than an apple. A young panda grows quickly, feeding on its mother's milk. When it is 20 weeks old it weighs more than 20 times its birth weight.

DO ANY FISH FEED THEIR YOUNG?

Yes – the discus fish lets its young feed on the sticky slime covering its body. Both the male and female feed their young in this way. Without this substance the young fish die, even if there is other food to eat. The discus fish lives in rivers in South America.

61

Questions and answers on dangerous animals

WHICH IS THE MOST POISONOUS FISH?

The deadly puffer fish is the most poisonous fish in the world. There is an extremely powerful poison in its heart, liver and other parts of its insides that can kill a person in two hours. Even though these fish are so deadly, they are a popular food in Japan. Specially trained chefs remove the poisonous parts of the body before cooking.

ARE THERE ANY POISONOUS MAMMALS?

Tiny shrews, and other shrewlike creatures called solenodons, are the only mammals with a poisonous bite. The shrew's poison is strong enough to kill a frog in just a few seconds. Another mammal, the duck-billed platypus, has a spur on each ankle. These are connected to poison glands in the legs. The platypus uses its poisonous spurs to protect itself from enemies, not to attack prey. The poison does not kill humans, but it does cause severe pain.

WHICH IS THE MOST DANGEROUS SHARK?

The great white shark is one of the fiercest flesh eaters in the ocean and has been known to attack people. However, these large creatures usually feed on fish – including other sharks – as well as seals and dolphins.

IS THERE REALLY A STING IN A SCORPION'S TAIL?

Scorpions do have a poisonous sting at the end of the body. They use the sting to paralyse the small creatures that they eat. The most poisonous scorpion of all lives in North Africa. It has a bite that can kill people.

WHICH IS THE MOST DANGEROUS JELLYFISH?

A jellyfish called the sea wasp is one of the world's most dangerous creatures. It has 40 million stinging cells on its tentacles and can kill a person in two or three minutes.

WHICH IS THE DEADLIEST SNAKE?

The sea snake, which lives in the Pacific Ocean, has a poison that is at least 100 times stronger than that of any land snake. Cobras and rattlesnakes are some of the most poisonous land snakes – one teaspoon of cobra poison could kill 80 people.

ARE ALL SPIDERS POISONOUS?

There are more than 35,000 different kinds of spiders and only about 30 are dangerous to people. One of the most poisonous is the black widow. This spider lives in North America and can kill a person with one bite. The funnel-web spider of Australia is also extremely deadly.

WHICH IS THE FIERCEST BIG CAT?

Lions, tigers and other big cats usually stay out of the way of humans, unless they are disturbed or frightened. But in an area of India called the Sundarbans there are some very dangerous tigers. Between 1975 and 1989 about 500 people were killed by tigers there.

ARE THERE ANY POISONOUS BIRDS?

The hooded pitohui lives in the jungles of New Guinea. Scientists have only recently discovered that it is poisonous. The feathers, skin and flesh of this bird contain a poison strong enough to kill frogs and mice. It causes numbness and sneezing in humans.

Puffer fish

WHICH IS THE MOST DANGEROUS BAT?

Most bats are not dangerous to people at all. But the vampire bat, which lives in the jungles of South America, bites animals such as cows, and even humans, to feed on their blood. As it feeds, the bat can pass on a deadly disease called rabies.

WHICH IS THE MOST POISONOUS FROG?

The golden arrow-poison frog is the most poisonous of all frogs. It has enough venom in its skin to kill more than 2,000 people. The arrow-poison frog lives in the jungles of South America. Local tribespeople use its poison to coat the tips of their hunting arrows and blow-pipe darts.

Questions and answers on nature's giants

WHICH IS THE BIGGEST CROCODILE?

At nearly six metres long, the estuarine crocodile is the biggest and probably the most dangerous crocodile. It lives in coastal seas and swamps in parts of Asia and Australia. It can swim long distances and does not spend much time on land.

WHICH IS THE BIGGEST LIZARD?

The Komodo dragon is about three metres long, much larger than any other lizard. It has a long tail, strong legs and sharp claws and it can catch animals as large as deer and wild boar. This lizard lives in Southeast Asia.

WHICH IS THE BIGGEST FROG?

The largest known frog is the rare goliath frog, which lives in Africa. It grows to about 36 centimetres long and weighs 3.5 kilograms – as much as a small domestic cat.

WHICH IS THE BIGGEST RODENT?

The biggest rodent is the capybara, which lives in South America. The capybara looks like a large, long-legged guinea pig, with a big head and square nose. It is a good swimmer and spends much of its life in water. It eats plants, including water plants.

WHICH IS THE LARGEST CRAB?

The giant spider crab, which lives in Japan, is the world's largest crab. Although its body is only about 45 centimetres long, its legs span more than 7.5 metres.

Estuarine crocodile

WHICH IS THE BIGGEST BEAR?

The Alaskan brown bear is the largest of the bears. Its body is about 2.5 metres long and it weighs up to 680 kilograms – more than the weight of ten adult humans. It catches fish and other animals but it also eats fruit, nuts and roots. The polar bear is nearly as big. It hunts seals and birds, as well as fish, in its Arctic home.

WHICH IS THE BIGGEST SEAL?

The huge southern elephant seal is the biggest of all seals. The male measures up to five metres long and weighs more 4,000 kilograms. Females are much smaller—only three metres long and 900 kilograms. Southern elephant seals live around Antarctica and eat fish and squid. The slightly smaller northern elephant seal lives along the west coast of North America.

HOW LONG IS THE LONGEST EARTHWORM?

The longest known earthworms live in southern Africa. The biggest worm ever found measured more than six metres.

WHICH IS THE BIGGEST FLYING BIRD?

The biggest bird of all is the ostrich, but it does not fly. The biggest flying bird is the great bustard. It is one metre long and weighs as much as 18 kilograms. It lives in parts of southern Europe and Asia and eats insects and seeds. The kori bustard, which lives in southern Africa, is almost as big.

WHICH IS THE BIGGEST SEABIRD?

The emperor penguin is the biggest penguin and the biggest of all seabirds. It stands 1.2 metres tall and weighs 40 kilograms. It lives in Antarctica and catches fish and squid to eat. The emperor also has the worst breeding conditions of any bird. The male keeps his partner's egg warm on his feet for two months during the dark Antarctic winter. He does not eat all this time.

WHICH IS THE LARGEST DEER?

The moose is the largest of all deer. Its body is three metres long and it has huge antlers. The moose eats plants and sometimes wades into water to feed on water plants. It lives in northern North America, Europe and Asia.

WHICH IS THE BIGGEST MONKEY?

The mandrill, which lives in Africa, is one of the biggest of all monkeys. It is about 90 centimetres long. Almost as big is the howler monkey, which lives in South American jungle. Its body is smaller than the mandrill's but it also has a 90-centimetre tail.

Questions and answers on animal eating habits

WHICH ANIMAL IS THE FUSSIEST EATER?

One of the fussiest eaters is the koala, which lives in Australia. The koala eats only the leaves of 12 types of eucalyptus tree, even though 100 different types of eucalyptus grow in Australia. The koala eats a lot of leaves – about a kilogram a day. Its body is specially adapted to this food and it cannot eat anything else.

Koala

HOW HUNGRY IS A CATERPILLAR?

From the moment it hatches until it is ready to turn into a butterfly, a caterpillar eats. During this time a caterpillar's weight can increase 2,000 or even 3,000 times. That is like a human baby growing up to be as heavy as two elephants!

HOW MUCH DOES A BLUE WHALE EAT?

Although it is so big, the blue whale is not a fierce hunter. It feeds mostly on small shrimplike creatures called krill. The whale filters these from the water through a special straining mechanism in its mouth. It can eat four tonnes of these creatures a day – that is about four million krill.

DO ANY CREATURES GROW THEIR OWN FOOD?

Some termites do, and so do leafcutting ants. The ants cut pieces of leaves and bring them to their nest where they chew them up into little pieces. The ants grow tiny fungi on the leaves, which they eat and feed to their young.

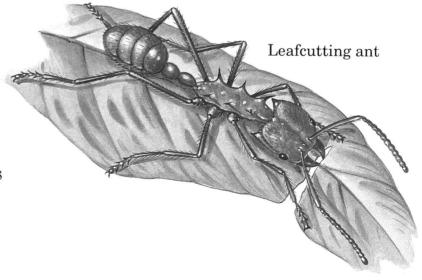

Leafcutting ant

66

HOW THIRSTY IS A CAMEL?

Camels live in the desert and are very good at surviving without water. They can last for several months without drinking at all. But when the camel does get near water it can swallow as much as 112 litres of water in a few minutes. The camel does not store water in its hump. The hump contains stores of fat, which build up when the camel has plenty of food to eat. At times when food is hard to find the camel lives off the fat in its hump.

DO ANIMALS USE TOOLS TO HELP THEM GET FOOD?

The sea otter is one of the few creatures that uses tools. It eats hard-shelled sea creatures, such as clams and sea urchins, which are too hard to crush with its teeth. So when the sea otter dives to find food, it also picks up a stone and brings it back to the surface. The otter lies on its back, holding the stone, and bangs the clam against it until the shell breaks. It can then feast on the soft flesh inside.

Blue whale

HOW MUCH DOES A HUMMINGBIRD EAT?

Hummingbirds feed on nectar – the sweet liquid made by flowers. As they feed, hummingbirds hover in front of flowers, moving their wings very fast. Hovering takes a lot of effort so hummingbirds need to feed every 10 or 15 minutes during the day to get enough energy. For a human to get the equivalent amount of energy, he or she would need to eat 130 loaves of bread or 370 pounds of potatoes.

DOES THE GIANT ANTEATER REALLY EAT ANTS?

It does – this strange long-nosed creature eats huge quantities of the insects, and their eggs and young. The anteater finds an ants' nest with the help of its powerful sense of smell. It breaks into the nest with its long claws and then scoops up lots of ants on its long, sticky tongue. The anteater can stretch its tongue out 60 centimetres so it can reach right into the nest.

Hummingbird

Questions and answers on animal behaviour

WHICH ANIMAL SHOUTS THE LOUDEST?

Howler monkeys are some of the world's noisiest land animals. The male has a special structure around the voice box, or larynx, in his throat. This makes his shouting calls echo and sound much louder. The monkeys shout to defend their territory, the area that they live in, against other rival monkeys. Their shouts can be heard as far as 16 kilometres away.

HOW LAZY IS A LION?

The mighty lion actually spends very little of its time hunting prey. Generally a lion spends up to 20 hours a day, resting and grooming. Lions are most active in the early morning and the late afternoon.

WHICH ANIMALS DIVE DEEPEST?

The sperm whale probably makes the deepest dives of any mammal. This huge whale regularly dives down to 1,000 metres and may even dive as deep as 3,000 metres. The whale dives to the depths of the ocean to find food, such as giant squid. It can stay under the water without taking a breath for 45 minutes.

Another deep diver is the Weddell seal. It plunges to 500 metres below the surface of the sea and can stay there for up to an hour before it has to come to the surface and take a breath.

ARE BEES REALLY BUSY?

Worker bees certainly are. Bees that live in large groups called colonies, such as honeybees, are divided into three types. In each colony there is a queen. She is the head of the colony and lays all the eggs. There are a few male drones who mate with the queen, but all the work is done by female worker bees. They build the nest and keep it clean. They also look after the young and guard the colony. Most important of all, workers gather nectar and pollen to make honey for food stores. A worker honeybee only lives six to eight weeks and has little time to rest.

Honeybee

WHY DO BIRDS SING?

Birds usually sing in spring, when it is time to look for a mate and make a nest. It is usually the male birds that sing to attract females. Once the breeding season is over, most birds stop singing. Birds also make simpler sounds when calling to each other or warning other birds of danger.

WHICH ANIMAL HIBERNATES FOR THE LONGEST?

Some animals sleep through the cold winter months. This sleep is called hibernation. As its hibernates, the animal's body temperature falls and its heart rate slows. This saves energy. Ground squirrels are among the animals that hibernate for longest. One Arctic ground squirrel hibernates for as long as seven or eight months.

WHICH ARE THE STRONGEST CREATURES?

Everyone knows that elephants are very strong, but, for their size, some beetles are even stronger. The rhinoceros beetle can carry more than 800 times its own weight on its back. An elephant can only carry about a quarter of its own body weight.

WHICH INSECT MAKES THE LOUDEST SOUND?

Male cicadas make the loudest calls of any insect. The sounds can be heard almost a kilometre away, even by humans. The sounds are made by special sheetlike structures at the sides of the body that are pushed in and out by muscles. Each movement makes a 'click'. The clicking calls of the male insects attract females.

HOW LONG DO ANIMALS LIVE?

It depends on the type of animal. Many insects live only a few weeks. The giant tortoise may live for 100 years. The Asian elephant is the longest lived mammal, apart from humans. It may live for 70 years. Small mammals, such as tiny mice and shrews live for only about 18 months.

DO YOUNG ANIMALS PLAY?

The young of larger mammals, such as cats, dogs and monkeys, do play. For many animals that have to hunt prey to eat, play is a part of their education. Adult lions and tigers bring injured prey to their young so they can practise making a kill. Fighting games with brothers and sisters teach a cub how to attack and defend itself. It will need these skills when it is grown up.

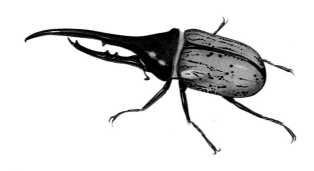

Index

A
airplane 48–49, 53
albatross, wandering 14–15
ant, leafcutting 66
anteater, giant 67
aphid 61
armadillo, giant 56

B
bat 55, 57
    long-eared 55
    vampire 63
bear
    brown 65
    polar 65
beaver 59
beetle
    click 40
    hercules 6–7
    rhinoceros 69
buffalo, water 56
bustard
    great 65
    kori 65
butterfly 8–9
    Cassius blue 8
    Queen Alexandra's
        birdwing 8–9
    red admiral 8–9
    Sonoran blue 8

C
camel 67
capybara 64
cat 22–23, 41, 43, 52, 69
caterpillar 66
cheetah 32–33, 52–53
chicken 50, 52
cicada 69
clam, giant 57
cobra 62
cockroach 38–39
crab, giant spider 64
crocodile, estuarine 64

D
deer 65
dog 55, 69
dolphin 56
    Commerson's 29
dove, rock 15
ducks 49, 60

E
eagle 60
    bald 16–17, 56
    golden 54
earthworm 65
eel, electric 54
egg 13
    bee hummingbird's 13
    hen's 13
    ostrich's 13
eider, common 48, 53
elephant 18, 28–29, 61
    African 26–27
    Asian 61, 69

F
falcon, peregrine 49, 53
fish
    discus 61
    labyrinth 58
    puffer 62
flea 41
frog
    golden arrow-poison 63
    goliath 64

G
giraffe 16–17, 24–25
goose 49
    spur-winged 48, 53
greyhound 30, 53

H
hare 30–31, 53
hen 60
honeybee 61, 68
human 30, 52
hummingbird 56, 67
    bee 12–13, 17
    ruby-throated 56

J
jellyfish 62

K
kangaroo 36–37
    grey 37, 52
    red 36
kiwi 55
koala 66
Komodo dragon 64

L
lion 63, 68, 69
lizard 64
    racerunner 43, 52

M
mallee fowl 59
mandrill 65
merganser 48, 52
mole 55
monkey 69
    howler 65, 68
moose 65
mouse, harvest 59

O
opossum, mouse 60
ostrich 12–13, 50–51, 52–53, 65
otter, sea 67
owl 55, 59
ox, musk 56

P
panda 61
partridge, grey 61
pelican, Australian 57
penguin
    emperor 65
    gentoo 44, 52
pheasant, argus 56
pig 26–27
pigeon 15
    racing 48, 53
piranha 54
pitohui, hooded 63
platypus, duck-billed 62
prairie dog 58
pronghorn 33, 52
python 60
    reticulated 20–21

R
racehorse 30–31, 53
roadrunner, greater 50, 52
robin 60

S
sailfish 44–45, 53
salmon 54
scorpion 62
seal
    northern elephant 65
    southern elephant 65
    Weddell 68
sea lion, Californian 45, 52
sea snake 62
sea wasp 62
shark 18–19, 54
    great white 18–19, 57, 62
    whale 18–19
shrew 62
sloth 34–35, 52
snail, garden 35
snake
    black mamba 42–43, 52
    sidewinder 42
spider 10–11
    black widow 63
    common house 11
    funnel-web 63
    goliath bird-eating 10–11
    wolf 60
springbok 37, 52
squid 46, 52
squirrel, Arctic ground 69
stick insect 6–7
submarine 44, 45, 53
sunspider 39, 52
swan, whistling 56

T
termite 58, 61, 66
tiger 22–23, 63, 69
tortoise
    giant 34, 52, 69
turtle
    green 59
    leatherback 44, 52

V
viper, gaboon 57
vole 61

W
whale 46
    blue 28–29, 66
    killer 46–47, 52
    sperm 68
windscorpion 39
windsurfer 47, 52
wrasse 58
wren 10